MENSA
CHALLENGE
YOUR IQ

THIS IS A CARLTON BOOK

Text & puzzle copyright © British Mensa Limited 1993
Design and artwork copyright © Carlton Books
Limited 1999

This Edition published by Carlton Books Limited 1999

A CIP catalogue for this book is available from the
British Library

ISBN 1 85868 311 4

Printed and bound in Great Britain

MENSA
CHALLENGE
YOUR IQ

Harold Gale & Carolyn Skitt

CARLTON

CONTENTS

AMERICAN MENSA

American Mensa Ltd is an organization for people who have one common trait: an IQ in the top 2% of the nation. Over 50,000 current members have found out how smart they are. This leaves room for an additional 4.5 million members in America alone. You may be one of them.

If you enjoy mental exercise, you'll find lots of good "workout programs" in the *Mensa Bulletin*, our national magazine. Voice your opinion in one of the newsletters published by each of our 150 local chapters. Learn from the many books and publications that are available to you as a member.

Are you a "people person," or would you like to meet other people with whom you feel comfortable? Then come to our local meetings, parties, and get-togethers. Participate in our lectures and debates. Attend our regional events and national gatherings. There's something happening on the Mensa calendar almost daily. So, you have lots of opportunities to meet people, exchange ideas, and make interesting new friends. Maybe you're looking for others who share your special interest? Whether yours is as common as crossword puzzles or as esoteric as Egyptology, there's a Mensa Special Interest Group (SIG) for it.

Take the challenge. Find out how smart you really are. Contact American Mensa Ltd today and ask for a free brochure. We enjoy adding new members and ideas to our high-IQ organization.

American Mensa Ltd,
1229 Corporate Drive West,
Arlington, TX 76006-6103.

Or, if you don't live in the USA and you'd like more details, you can contact Mensa International, 15 The Ivories, 628 Northampton Street, London N1 2NY, England, who will be happy to put you in touch with your own national Mensa.

INTRODUCTION

Intelligence, to a greater or lesser degree, is found in all humans. Your level of intelligence is the same throughout your life. Many people fail to discover their true potential however. It can be fun to challenge your IQ.

The tests in this book are fun IQ tests. They begin on an easy plane but gradually rise to a more difficult one. The tests measure speed and accuracy of thought and should be regarded as a form of mental jogging. Many people take physical exercise, but fewer take mental exercise. Now is your chance.

The tests in this book aren't to be taken too seriously though, as IQ can only be properly evaluated with accurate standardized tests in a scientific environment. The answers in this book will tell you your fun IQ, not your actual one. If you do well at these puzzles—or even if you don't—why not get in contact with Mensa and have your IQ accurately rated? You might surprise yourself...

R. P. Allen

Robert Allen,
Editorial Director,
Mensa Publications.

TEST 1

1 Which of the numbers should replace the question mark?

TEST 1 time limit 20 minutes

A	B	C	D
3	5	1	9
2	0	4	6
7	1	0	8
2	3	1	?

8 **A**	2 **B**
9 **C**	1 **D**
4 **E**	6 **F**

TEST 1

2 Each same symbol has a value. Work out the logic and discover what should replace the question mark.

TEST 1 time limit 20 minutes

Z	Z	Ψ	Ω	**?**
Ξ	Ξ	Ξ	Ξ	**8**
Ψ	Z	Ψ	Ω	**16**
Ψ	Z	Ψ	Ξ	**13**
13	**11**	**14**	**14**	

6	A	12	B	7	C

15	D	10	E	9	F

TEST 1

3 Here is an unusual safe. Each of the buttons must be pressed only once in the correct order to open it. The last button is marked F. The number of moves and the direction is marked on each button. Thus 1U would mean one move up, while 1L would mean one move to the left. Using the grid reference, which button is the first you must press?

TEST 1 time limit 20 minutes

	A	B	C	D	E
	3R	4D	2L	2L	2D
	3R	3R	3D	2L	2D
	1R	1D	F	3L	2L
	2U	1L	3U	1U	2L
	4R	1L	1R	1U	4U

5D	3C
A	**B**

1A	4E
C	**D**

1B	2C
E	**F**

TEST 1

4 Insert the correct mathematical signs between each number in order to resolve the equation. What are the signs?

| 11 | | 3 | | 7 | = | 21 |

A − +

B + −

C ✗ +

D ✗ −

E + +

F − −

TEST 1

5 Which triangle continues this series?

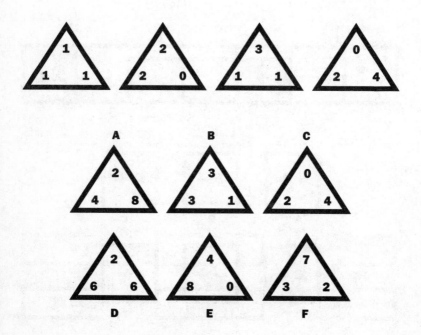

TEST 1

6 Discover the connection between the letters and the numbers. Which number should replace the question mark?

G	7
M	13
U	21
J	10
W	?

14	23	9
A	B	C
26	2	11
D	E	F

TEST 1

7 Which of the constructed boxes cannot be made from the pattern?

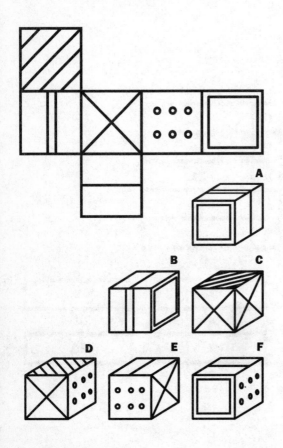

TEST 1

8 Which of the numbers should replace the question mark?

TEST 1 time limit 20 minutes

3	4	1	2
5	2	2	1
1	1	1	7
1	2	6	?

3 A	**5** B
1 C	**6** D
2 E	**4** F

15

TEST 1

9 Which of the clocks continues this series?

TEST 1 time limit 20 minutes

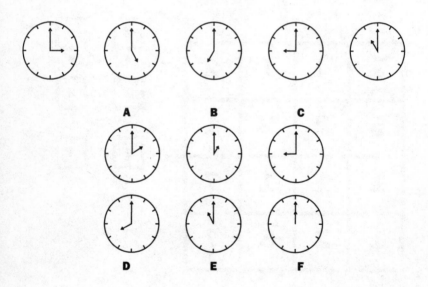

TEST 1

10 When rearranged the shapes will give a number. Which of the numbers is it?

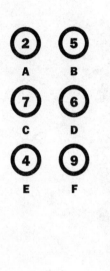

A ② **B** ⑤
C ⑦ **D** ⑥
E ④ **F** ⑨

TEST 1

11 Move from ring to touching ring, starting from the bottom left corner and finishing in the top right corner. Collect nine numbers and total them. Which is the highest possible total?

TEST 1 time limit 20 minutes

TEST 1

12 This square follows a logical pattern. Which of the tiles should be used to complete the square?

3	2	3	3	
2	2	3	2	
3	3	2	3	2
3	2	3	2	2
2	2	2	2	3

1	3
4	1
A	**B**

2	2
3	2
C	**D**

3	3
2	4
E	**F**

TEST 1

13 Which of the slices should be used to complete the cake?

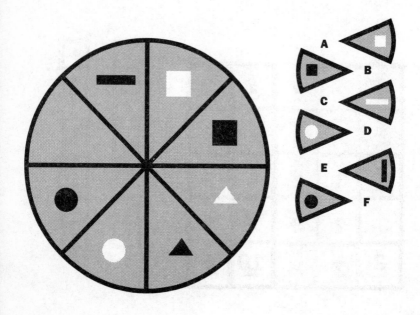

TEST 1

14 Each straight line of five numbers should total 20. Which of the numbers will replace the question mark?

TEST 1 time limit 20 minutes

5	2		2	5
1		?		1
5	8	4		3
	2	2	2	8
3	2	2	10	3

4 A	**1** B
3 C	**6** D
5 E	**2** F

21

TEST 1

15 Start at any corner and follow the lines. Collect another four numbers and total the five. One of the numbers in the squares below can be used to complete the diagram. If the correct one has been chosen, one of the routes involving it will give a total of 28. Which one is it?

TEST 1 time limit 20 minutes

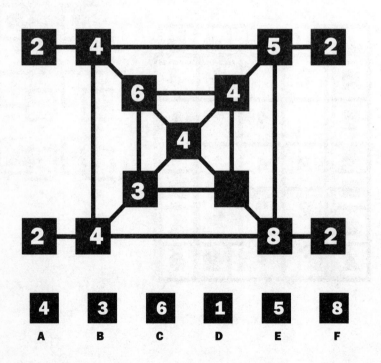

TEST 2

1 Which of the boxes should be used to replace the question mark?

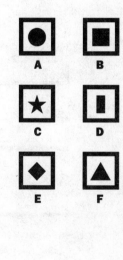

TEST 2

2 Scales one and two are in perfect balance. Which of these pans should replace the empty one?

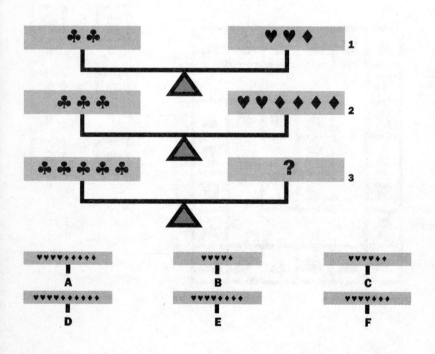

TEST 2

3 How many ways are there to score 25 on this dartboard using three darts only? Each dart always lands in a sector and no dart falls to the floor.

TEST 2 time limit 20 minutes

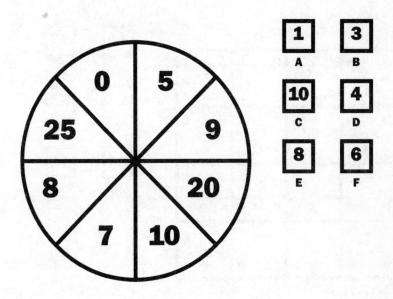

TEST 2

4 Which square's contents matches D1?

TEST 2 time limit 20 minutes

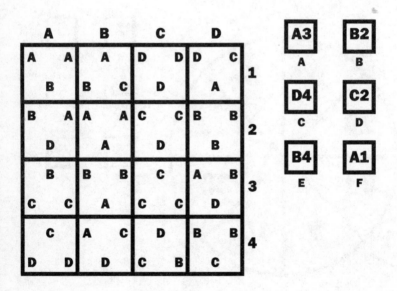

TEST 2

5 Which of the numbers should logically replace the question mark in the octagon?

TEST 2 time limit 20 minutes

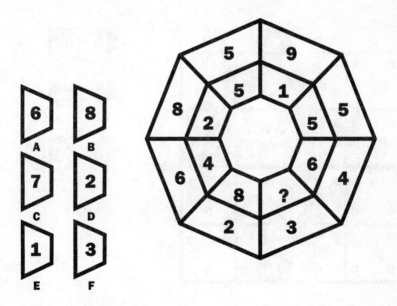

TEST 2

6 Which number is missing from this series?

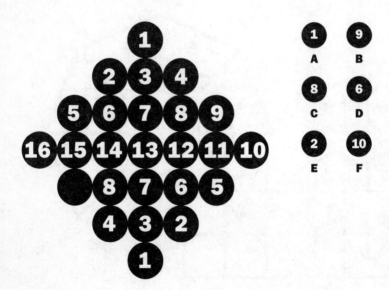

A 1
B 9
C 8
D 6
E 2
F 10

TEST 2

7   Complete the square using the five numbers shown. When completed no row, column or diagonal line will use the same number more than once. What should replace the question mark?

1	2	3	4	5
4	5	1	2	3
?				

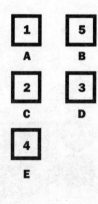

1   5
A   B

2   3
C   D

4
E

TEST 2

8 Which of the numbers should replace the question mark?

TEST 2 time limit 20 minutes

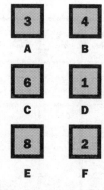

6	3	1	4	9
5	1	0	2	8
1	2	1	2	?

TEST 2

9 Start at 1 and move from circle to touching circle. Collect four numbers each time. How many different routes are there to collect 11? A reversed route counts twice.

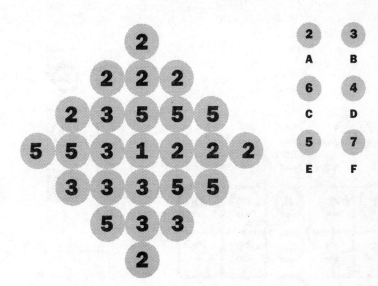

TEST 2

10 Here is an unusual safe. Each of the buttons must be pressed only once in the correct order to open it. The last button is marked F. The number of moves and the direction is marked on each button. Thus 1i would mean one move in, whilst 1o would mean one move out. 1c would mean one move clockwise and 1a would mean one move anti-clockwise. Which button is the first you must press?

TEST 2 time limit 20 minutes

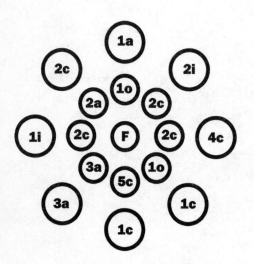

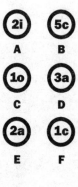

TEST 2

11 Which of the numbers should replace the question mark?

6	3	1	8
5	4	2	7
0	9	4	5
7	2	8	?

6 A	**3** W
2 C	**4** D
1 E	**5** F

TEST 2

12 Which triangle continues this series?

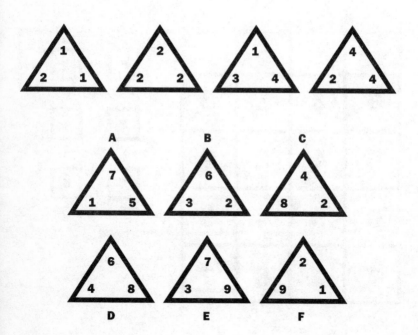

TEST 2

13 Insert the correct mathematical signs between each number in order to resolve the equation. What are the signs?

| **13** | | **2** | | **4** | **=** | **7** |

+ −
A

✕ +
B

− −
C

✕ ✕
D

÷ ✕
E

− ✕
F

TEST 2

14 Discover the connection between the letters and the numbers. Which number should replace the question mark?

C	3	14	N
Y	25	12	L
F	6	19	S
U	21	16	P
O			D

15	4

A

5	26

B

11	18

C

24	8

D

13	3

E

1	19

F

TEST 2

15 Which of the constructed boxes can be made from the pattern?

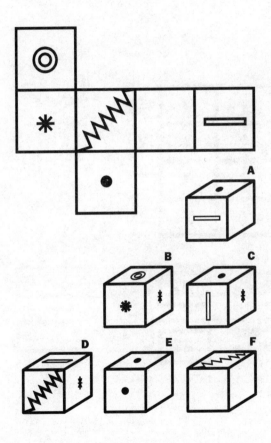

TEST 3

1 Each same symbol has a value.
Work out the logic and discover what
should replace the question mark.

α	α	α	α	16
β	β	δ	χ	?
δ	α	δ	α	
α	β	χ	χ	21
	22	25		

25 A		**21** B		**27** C	
28 D		**29** E		**23** F	

TEST 3

2 Scales one and two are in perfect balance. Which of these pans should replace the empty one?

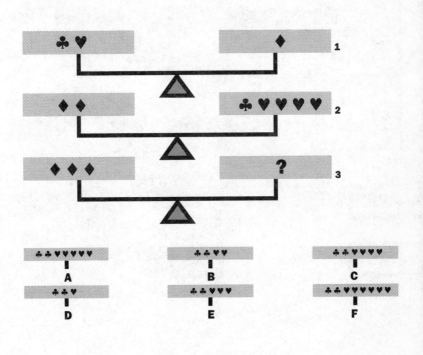

TEST 3

3 When rearranged the shapes will give a number. Which of the numbers is it?

6 — A

7 — B

9 — C

3 — D

8 — E

4 — F

TEST 3

4 Which of the numbers should replace the question mark?

TEST 3 time limit 25 minutes

6	1	7	3
2	5	2	8
3	5	5	1
4	4	1	?

6 A	3 B
4 C	2 D
5 E	1 F

TEST 3

5 Here is an unusual safe. Each of the buttons must be pressed only once in the correct order to open it. The last button is marked F. The number of moves and the direction is marked on each button. Thus 1i would mean one move in, whilst 1o would mean one move out. 1c would mean one move clock-wise and 1a would mean one move anti-clockwise. Which button is the first you must press?

TEST 3 time limit 25 minutes

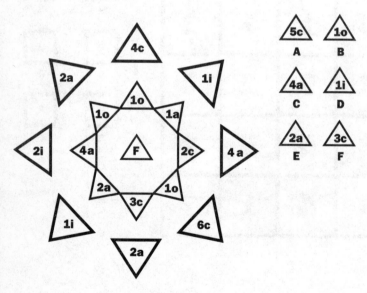

TEST 3

6 Which number is missing from this series?

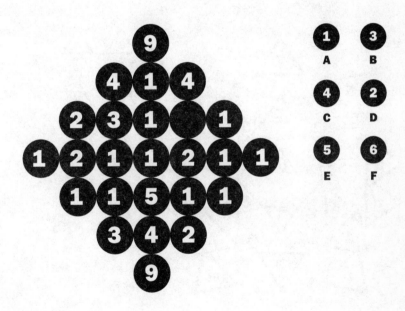

TEST 3

7 Which triangle should replace the empty one?

TEST 3

8 Which of the numbers should logically replace the question mark in the octagon?

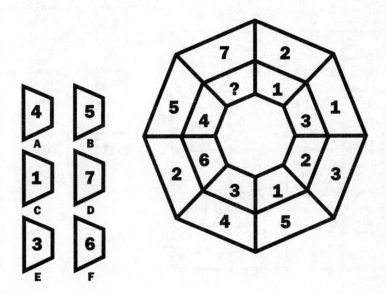

TEST 3

9 Which square's contents matches C4?

TEST 3 time limit 25 minutes

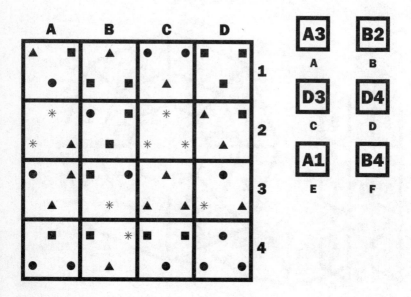

TEST 3

10 How many ways are there to score 123 on this dartboard using three darts only? Each dart always lands in a sector and no dart falls to the floor. Any sector can be used more than once in any set of throws, but the same set of numbers can be used in one order only.

TEST 3 time limit 25 minutes

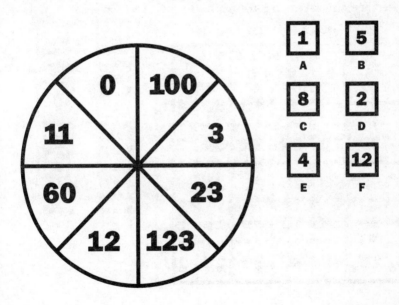

TEST 3

TEST 3 time limit 25 minutes

11 Here is an unusual safe. Each of the buttons must be pressed only once in the correct order to open it. The last button is marked F. The number of moves and the direction is marked on each button. Thus 1U would mean one move up, while 1L would mean one move to the left. Using the grid reference, which button is the first you must press?

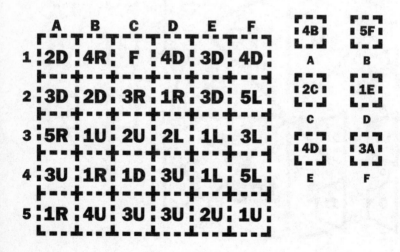

	A	B	C	D	E	F
1	2D	4R	F	4D	3D	4D
2	3D	2D	3R	1R	3D	5L
3	5R	1U	2U	2L	1L	3L
4	3U	1R	1D	3U	1L	5L
5	1R	4U	3U	3U	2U	1U

4B	5F
A	B

2C	1E
C	D

4D	3A
E	F

TEST 3

12 Which of the numbers should logically replace the question mark in the octagon?

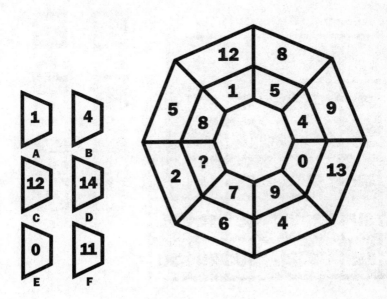

TEST 3

13 Which of the numbers should
replace the question mark?

1	0	3	4
8	4	2	6
6	2	3	7
9	5	2	?

6 **A**	9 **B**
5 **C**	3 **D**
2 **E**	7 **F**

TEST 3

14 Which of the boxes should be
used to replace the question mark?

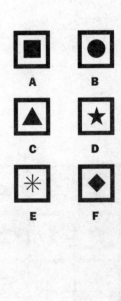

TEST 3

15 Which of the numbers should replace the question mark?

2	1	2	1	?
5	1	2	7	3
7	2	4	8	6

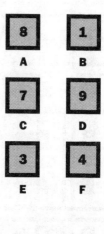

8
A

1
B

7
C

9
D

3
E

4
F

TEST 3

16 This square follows a logical pattern. Which of the tiles should be used to complete the square?

TEST 3 time limit 25 minutes

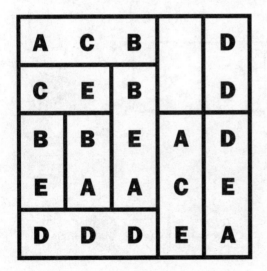

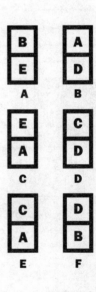

TEST 3

17 Which of the constructed boxes cannot be made from the pattern?

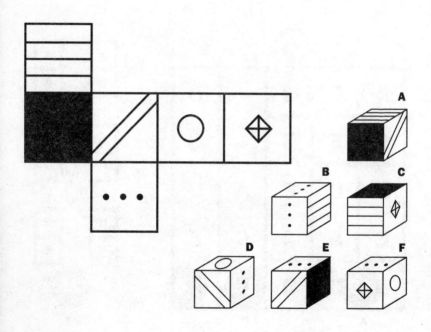

TEST 3

18 Move from ring to touching ring, starting from the bottom left corner and finishing in the top right corner. Collect nine numbers and total them. Which is the highest possible total

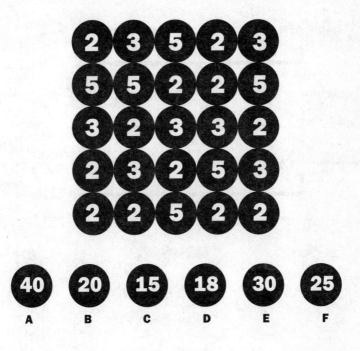

2 3 5 2 3
5 5 2 2 5
3 2 3 3 2
2 3 2 5 3
2 2 5 2 2

40 20 15 18 30 25
A   B   C   D   E   F

TEST 3

19 Scales one and two are in perfect balance. Which of the pans should replace the empty one?

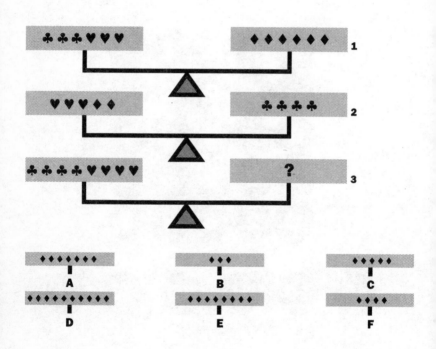

TEST 3

20 Which of the clocks continues this series?

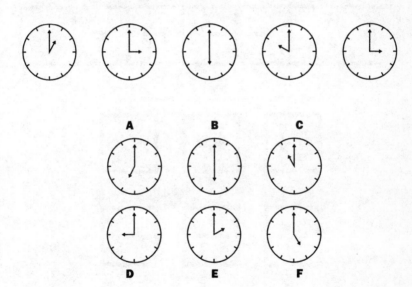

TEST 4

1 Insert the correct mathematical signs between each number in order to resolve the equation. What are the signs?

TEST 4 time limit 25 minutes

| 9 | | 3 | | 17 | = | 44 |

A × +

B + ×

C − ×

D ÷ −

E + ÷

F + +

TEST 4

2 Start at 1 and move from circle to touching circle. Collect four numbers each time. How many different routes are there to collect 12? A reversed route counts twice.

```
            2
         3  3  2
      3  6  6  6  2
   6  2  3  1  3  6  3
      3  6  2  3  3
         6  6  2
            2
```

12 A	**9** B
8 C	**7** D
11 E	**3** F

TEST 4

3 Which triangle belongs to this series?

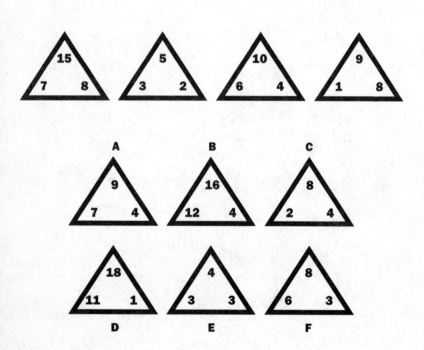

TEST 4

4 Which of the clocks continues this series?

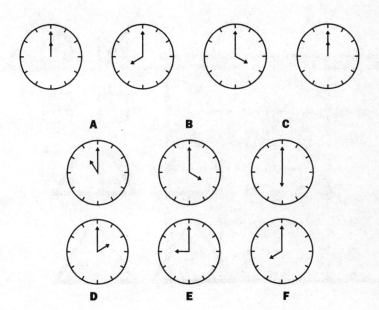

TEST 4

5 Which of the numbers should replace the question mark?

	A	B	C	D
	7	9	8	8
	3	9	5	7
	1	6	3	4
	2	2	1	?

4	2
A	**B**

3	1
C	**D**

5	6
E	**F**

TEST 4

6 Here is an unusual safe. Each of the buttons must be pressed only once in the correct order to open it. The last button is marked F. The number of moves and the direction is marked on each button. Thus 1U would mean one move up, while 1L would mean one move to the left. Using the grid reference, which button is the first you must press?

	A	B	C	D	E
1	2R	2R	4D	1D	4L
2	1D	1U	F	3D	3L
3	3R	1R	1D	1R	3L
4	4R	1D	1R	2L	3U
5	1U	3R	3U	3L	3U

2C	1E
A	B

4D	3E
C	D

2A	5B
E	F

TEST 4

7 Start at any corner and follow the lines. Collect another four numbers and total the five. One of the numbers in the squares below can be used to complete the diagram. If the correct one has been chosen, one of the routes involving it will give a total of 33. Which one is it?

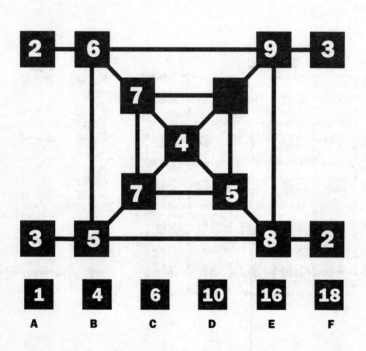

TEST 4

8 This square follows a logical pattern. Which of the tiles should be used to complete the square?

TEST 4 time limit 25 minutes

5	3	1	3	1
3	5	5	1	5
	5	3	1	5
	1	1	3	5
1	5	5	5	3

1 3	5 2
A	**B**
3 5	5 1
C	**D**
1 2	1 1
E	**F**

TEST 4

9 Move from ring to touching ring, starting from the bottom left corner and finishing in the top right corner. Collect nine numbers and total them. Which is the highest possible total?

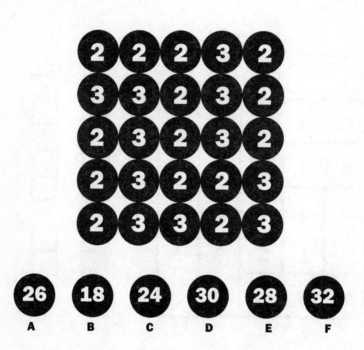

TEST 4

10 When rearranged the shapes will give a number. Which of the numbers is it?

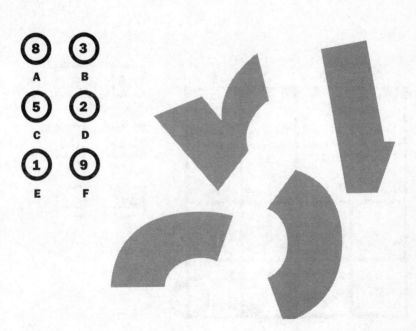

8 A

3 B

5 C

2 D

1 E

9 F

TEST 4

Which square's contents matches
D1?

TEST 4 time limit 25 minutes

	A		B		C		D	
1	3 3		2		2		4	
	2		1 1	2 2	2 1	
2	4 4		2		2		3 3	
	3		4 4	4 1	4	
3	3		3		1		4 4	
	2 2	1 1	3 3	4	
4	3		2 2	1		2 2	
	3 3	4	1 1	1	

A4 — A

B2 — B

C1 — C

C2 — D

A1 — E

D3 — F

68

TEST 4

12 How many ways are there to score 60 on this dartboard using three darts only? Each dart always lands in a sector and no dart falls to the floor.

TEST 4 time limit 25 minutes

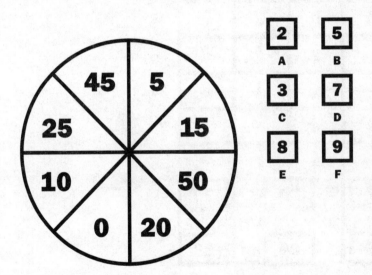

2	5
A	B

3	7
C	D

8	9
E	F

TEST 4

13 Each same symbol has a value. Work out the logic and discover what should replace the question mark.

TEST 4 time limit 25 minutes

α	β	α	β	18
β	χ	δ	α	
χ	χ	β	β	20
χ	δ	δ	δ	?
23			22	

37 A   **30** B   **28** C

35 D   **24** E   **39** F

TEST 4

14 Which of the boxes should be used to replace the question mark?

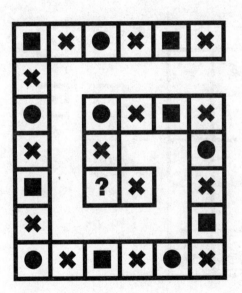

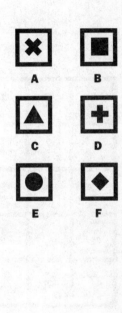

A

B

C

D

E

F

TEST 4

15 Complete the square using the five numbers shown. When completed no row, column or diagonal line will use the same number more than once. What should replace the question mark?

TEST 4 time limit 25 minutes

1	2	3	4	5
		5		
?		2		
		4		
4	5	1	2	3

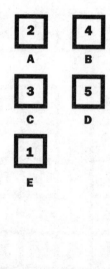

2		4
A		B

3		5
C		D

1	
E	

TEST 4

16 Which circle should replace the empty one?

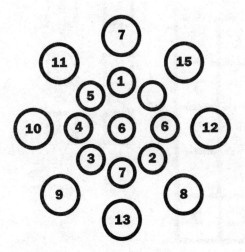

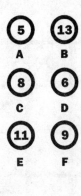

TEST 4

17 Each straight line of five numbers should total 25. Which of the numbers will replace the question mark?

TEST 4 time limit 25 minutes

?	2		1	
2		7		1
			1	2
4	2	3	3	
3	5	3	12	2

8	6
A	**B**

12	10
C	**D**

2	15
E	**F**

TEST 4

18 Which of the slices should be used to replace the question mark and complete the cake?

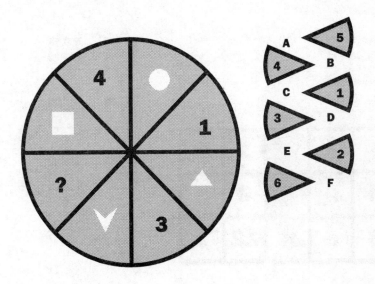

TEST 4

19 Which of the numbers should replace the question mark?

5	9	1	2	1
8	9	6	4	3
3	0	5	2	?

9	6
A	B
2	7
C	D
4	5
E	F

TEST 4

20 Discover the connection between the letters and the numbers. Which number should replace the question mark?

S	?	K
E	516	P
Z	262	B
I	914	N
A	120	T

393	**671**	**385**
A	B	C
5482	**1911**	**2363**
D	E	F

TEST 5

1   Here is an unusual safe. Each of the buttons must be pressed only once in the correct order to open it. The last button is marked F. The number of moves and the direction is marked on each button. Thus 1i would mean one move in, while 1o would mean one move out. 1c would mean one move clock-wise and 1a would mean one move anti-clockwise. Which button is the first you must press?

TEST 5 time limit 40 minutes

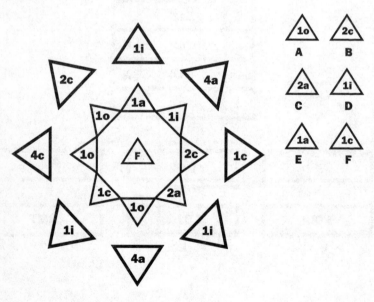

TEST 5

2 Complete the square using the five symbols shown. When completed no row, column or diagonal line will use the same symbol more than once. What should replace the question mark?

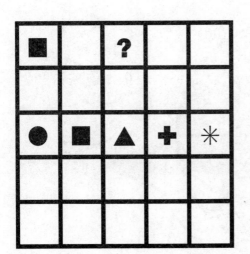

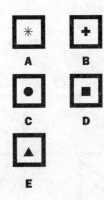

A   B

C   D

E

TEST 5

3 Which of the slices should be used to complete the cake?

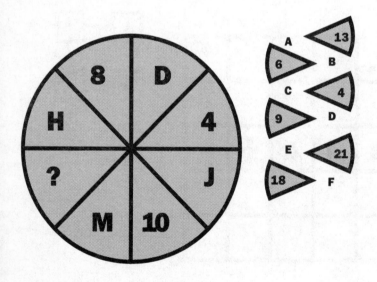

TEST 5

4 Start at 4 and move from circle to touching circle. Collect four numbers each time. How many different routes are there to collect 24? A reversed route counts twice.

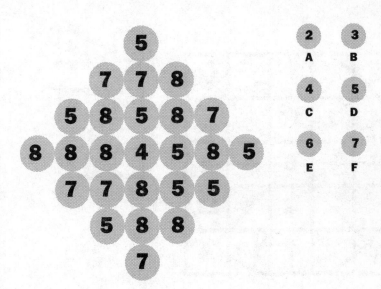

TEST 5

5 Each straight line of five numbers should total 30. Which of the numbers will replace the question mark?

TEST 5 time limit 40 minutes

8				10
4	7	10		
7	8	6	4	5
		2	5	11
2		?	12	4

15	13
A	B

19	14
C	D

16	3
E	F

TEST 5

6 Which number is missing from this series?

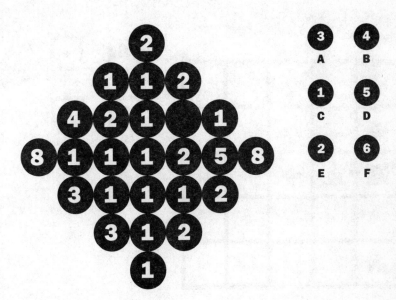

TEST 5

7 Complete the square using the five symbols shown. When completed no row, column or diagonal line will use the same symbol more than once. What should replace the question mark?

TEST 5 time limit 40 minutes

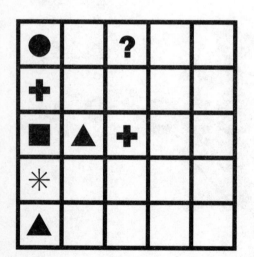

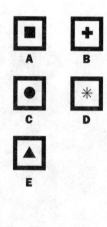

TEST 5

8 Which triangle should replace the empty one?

TEST 5 time limit 40 minutes

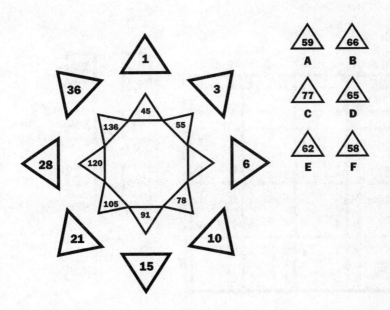

TEST 5

9 Which square's contents matches C1?

TEST 5 time limit 40 minutes

	A	B	C	D	
	A E B D	A A A A	A A B D	B B A B	**1**
	D E B B	E E E E	B C E A	B B B C	**2**
	D D A D	C A C B	C C E E	A B C D	**3**
	B E D C	A E E D	B A A D	D D C D	**4**

4A A	**2D** B
4C C	**1B** D
3B E	**1D** F

TEST 5

10 How many ways are there to score 62 on this dartboard using four darts only? Each dart always lands in a sector and no dart falls to the floor.

TEST 5 time limit 40 minutes

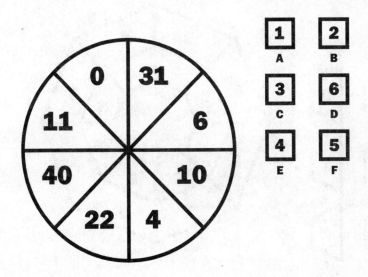

TEST 5

11 Which of the numbers should logically replace the question mark in the octagon?

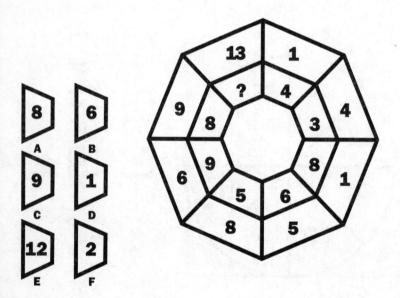

TEST 5

12 This square follows a logical pattern. Which of the tiles should be used to complete the square?

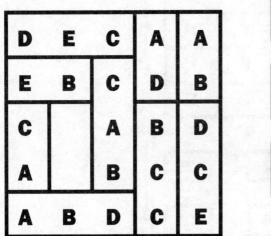

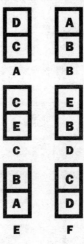

TEST 5

13 Each letter has a value. Work out the logic and discover what should replace the question mark.

TEST 5 time limit 40 minutes

A	B	C	D	5
E	F	G	H	11
I	J	K	L	32
M	N	O	P	?
22	**14**	**20**	**30**	

45	A	12	B	26	C
38	D	34	E	21	F

TEST 5

14 Here is an unusual safe. Each of the buttons must be pressed only once in the correct order to open it. The last button is marked F. The number of moves and the direction is marked on each button. Thus 1U would mean one move up, while 1L would mean one move to the left. Using the grid reference, which button is the first you must press?

	A	B	C	D	E	F
1	4D	3R	3D	2R	4L	3L
2	3R	3R	1L	3D	1D	5L
3	1R	2D	1U	1L	4L	1D
4	1R	2R	1D	1U	4L	2U
5	4R	4U	F	4U	1R	2U

2F	5C
A	B

4D	5B
C	D

4E	3F
E	F

TEST 5

15 Move from ring to touching ring, starting from the bottom left corner and finishing in the top right corner. Collect nine numbers and total them. Which is the highest possible total?

TEST 5 time limit 40 minutes

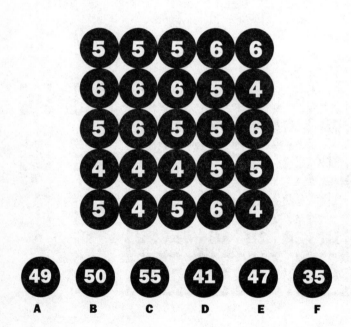

TEST 5

16 Which of the numbers should replace the question mark?

A	B	C	D
8	3	4	1
6	1	2	3
9	2	0	7
5	1	1	?

7	4
A	B
1	6
C	D
3	9
E	F

TEST 5

17 Start at any corner and follow the lines. Collect another four numbers and total the five. One of the numbers in the squares below can be used to complete the diagram. If the correct one has been chosen, one of the routes involving it will give a total of 20. Which one is it?

TEST 5 time limit 40 minutes

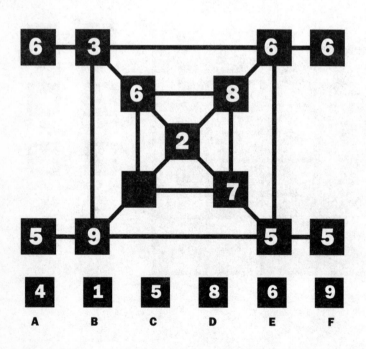

TEST 5

18 Scales one and two are in perfect balance. Which of these pans should replace the empty one?

TEST 5 time limit 40 minutes

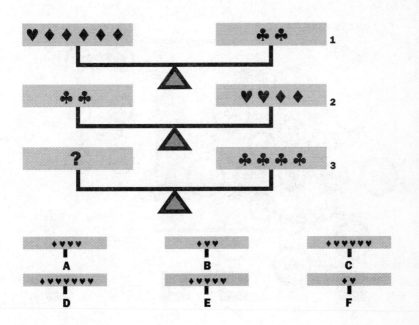

TEST 5

19   Here is an unusual safe. Each of the buttons must be pressed only once in the correct order to open it. The last button is marked F. The number of moves and the direction is marked on each button. Thus 1i would mean one move in, while 1o would mean one move out. 1c would mean one move clock-wise and 1a would mean one move anti-clockwise. Which button is the first you must press?

TEST 5 time limit 40 minutes

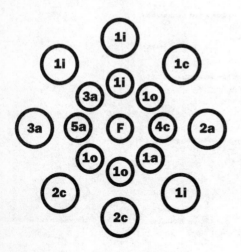

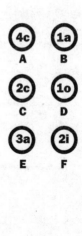

TEST 5

20 Insert the correct mathematical signs between each number in order to resolve the equation. What are the signs?

TEST 5 time limit 40 minutes

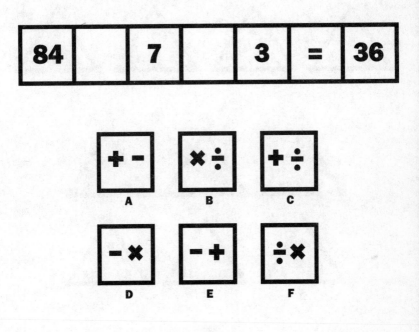

TEST 5

21 Which triangle belongs to this series?

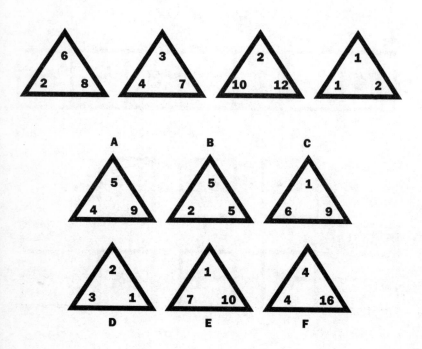

TEST 5

22 Discover the connection between the letters and the numbers. Which number should replace the question mark?

C	23	T
J	17	G
L	34	V
E	10	E
A	?	X

13	21	25
A	B	C
33	26	28
D	E	F

TEST 5

23 Which of the clocks continues this series?

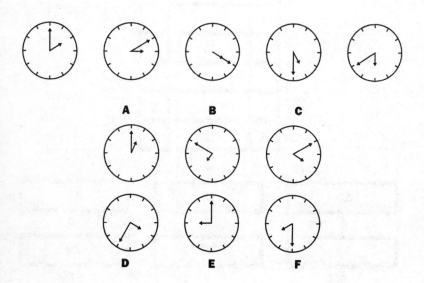

A   B   C

D   E   F

TEST 5

24 Which of the numbers should replace the question mark?

9	7	8	5
3	1	4	3
8	8	7	6
2	2	3	?

1 A	6 B
2 C	5 D
3 E	4 F

TEST 5

25 Which of the constructed boxes can be made from the pattern?

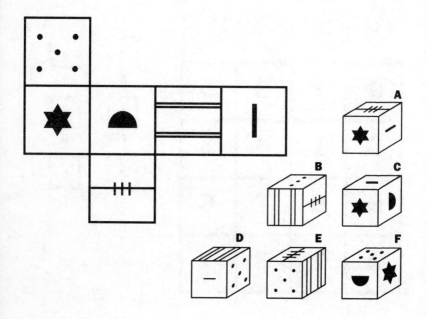

TEST 5

26 When rearranged the shapes will give a letter. Which of the letters is it?

R
A

D
B

K
C

J
D

L
E

S
F

TEST 5

27 Start at 4 and move from circle to touching circle. Collect four numbers each time. How many different routes are there to collect 10? A reversed route counts twice.

TEST 5 time limit 40 minutes

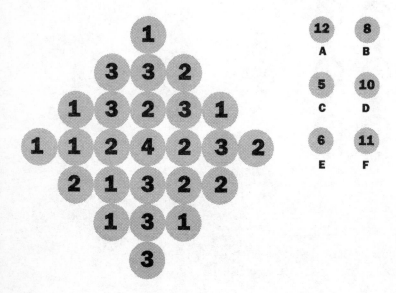

TEST 5

28 Each straight line of five numbers should total 50. Which of the numbers will replace the question mark?

12	10	14		12
7	14	14	14	1
12	18			8
11			?	21
8	2		26	8

6 **A**	4 **B**
12 **C**	10 **D**
8 **E**	2 **F**

TEST 5

29 Which of the boxes should be used to replace the question mark?

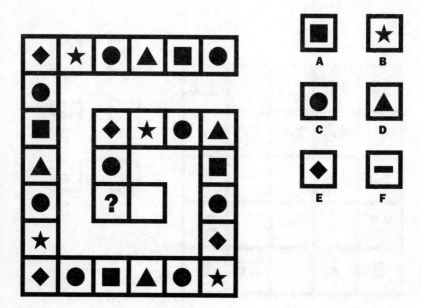

TEST 5

30 Each straight line of five numbers should total 35. Only two numbers must be used to complete the square. Which of the numbers will replace the question mark?

TEST 5 time limit 40 minutes

9	8	11	0	
1	11	11	9	
	11	?		
11	5			13
	0		20	5

12 A	**9** B
1 C	**10** D
7 E	**4** F

TEST 6

1 Which of the slices should be used to complete the cake?

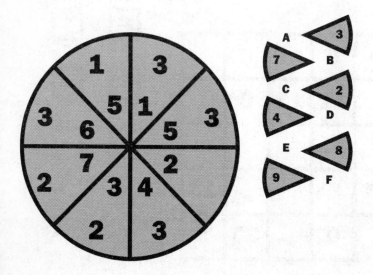

TEST 6

2 Start at any corner and follow the lines. Collect another four numbers and total the five. One of the numbers in the squares below can be used to complete the diagram. If the correct one has been chosen, one of the routes involving it will give a total of 41. Which one is it?

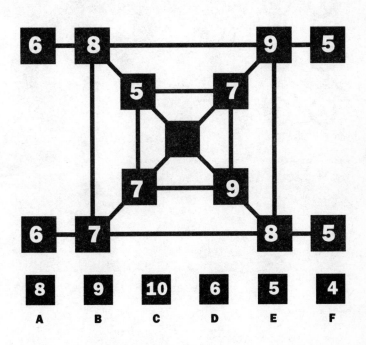

TEST 6

3 When rearranged the shapes will give a letter. Which of the letters is it?

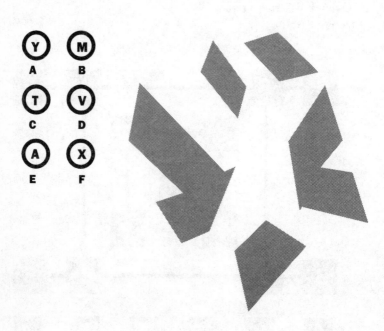

4 Each straight line of five numbers should total 40. Only two numbers are used to complete the square. Which of the numbers will replace the question mark?

TEST 6 time limit 45 minutes

			2	
12				0
	?	8	6	6
3	7	6	7	17
6	5	6	16	7

4 A	**10** B
13 C	**21** D
18 E	**5** F

TEST 6

5 Here is an unusual safe. Each of the buttons must be pressed only once in the correct order to open it. The last button is marked F. The number of moves and the direction is marked on each button. Thus 1i would mean one move in, while 1o would mean one move out. 1c would mean one move clockwise and 1a would mean one move anti-clockwise. Which button is the first you must press?

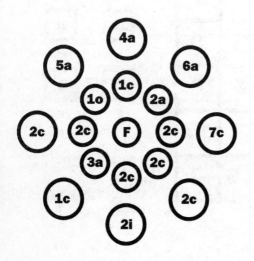

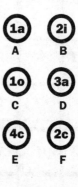

112

TEST 6

6 Scales one and two are in perfect balance. Which of these pans should replace the empty one?

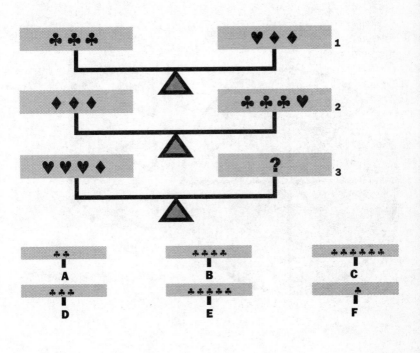

113

TEST 6

7 Which of the slices should be used to complete the cake?

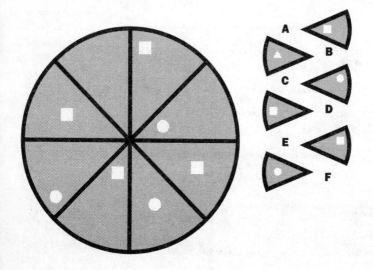

TEST 6

8 Which of the numbers should replace the question mark?

6	3	9	4	1
5	8	7	6	3
?	5	1	7	8

3	5
A	B

8	7
C	D

2	0
E	F

TEST 6

9 Which arrow is missing from this series?

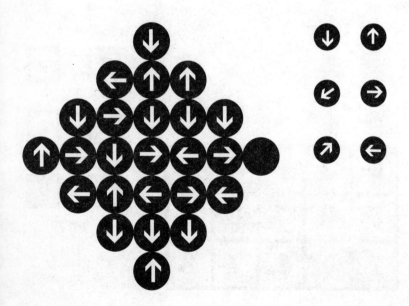

TEST 6

10 Move from ring to touching ring, starting from the bottom left corner and finishing in the top right corner. Collect nine numbers and total them. Which is the highest possible total?

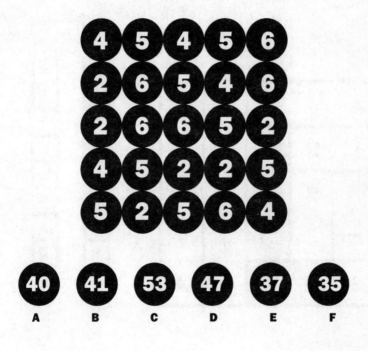

TEST 6

11 This square follows a logical pattern. Which of the tiles should be used to complete the square?

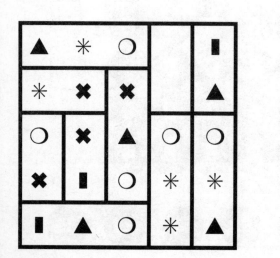

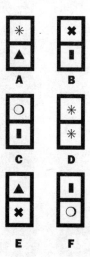

TEST 6

 Which square's contents matches D4?

	A		B		C		D	
1	1	1	5	1	3	1	1	3
	5	5	2	3	2	3	5	4
2	2	3	4	4	4	2	3	3
	4	3	1	4	2	5	4	5
3	3	3	1	4	4	4	2	5
	4	3	2	5	1	1	4	3
4	3	4	5	3	4	2	3	5
	2	2	4	4	3	1	1	2

A2 A

C1 B

D3 C

C3 D

B4 E

B1 F

TEST 6

13 How many ways are there to score 85 on this dartboard using four darts only? Each dart always lands in a sector and no dart falls to the floor.

TEST 6 time limit 45 minutes

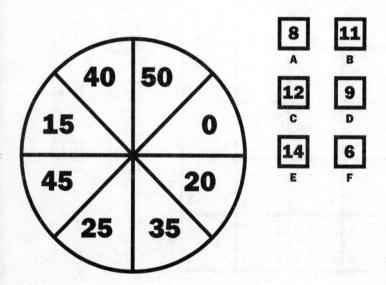

8 A	**11** B
12 C	**9** D
14 E	**6** F

TEST 6

14 Which of the numbers should logically replace the question mark in the octagon?

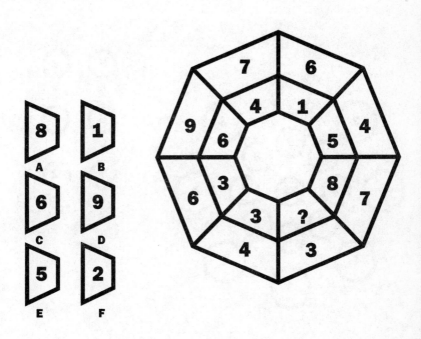

TEST 6

15 Which circle should replace the empty one?

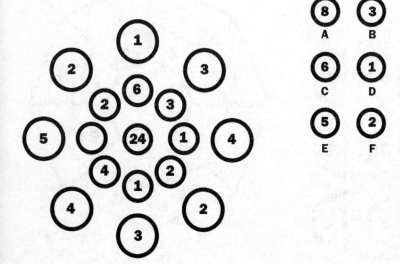

TEST 6

16 Complete the square using the five numbers shown. When completed no row, column or diagonal line will use the same number more than once. What should replace the question mark?

1	2			
4	5			
2	3			
				?

4 A	**5** B
1 C	**2** D
3 E	

TEST 6

17 Discover the connection between the letters and the numbers. Which number should replace the question mark?

A	1	B
D	7	K
Q	2	O
R	2	T
Z	?	C

12	5	20
A	B	C

28	23	9
D	E	F

TEST 6

18 Which triangle belongs to this series?

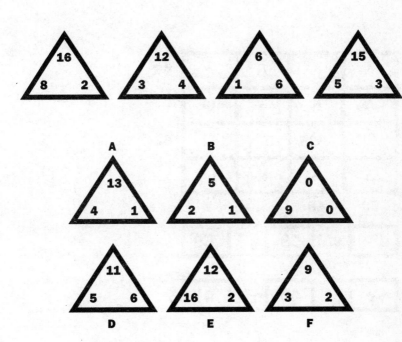

125

TEST 6

19 Each same symbol has a value. Work out the logic and discover what should replace the question mark.

TEST 6 time limit 45 minutes

K	K	Λ	Λ	46
Λ	K	K	O	
O	O	Π	Π	62
Λ	Λ	K	O	

50   49   ?

48	A	58	B	50	C
42	D	49	E	47	F

TEST 6

20 Which of the numbers should replace the question mark?

2	3	2	8
1	8	1	9
3	0	3	3
1	1	4	?

2 **A**	1 **B**
4 **C**	5 **D**
8 **E**	7 **F**

TEST 6

21 Which of the clocks continues this series?

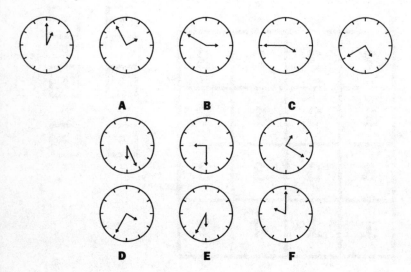

A   B   C

D   E   F

TEST 6

22 Which of the constructed boxes cannot be made from the pattern?

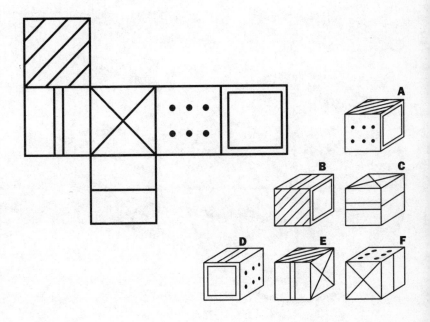

TEST 6

23 Which of the slices should be used to complete the cake?

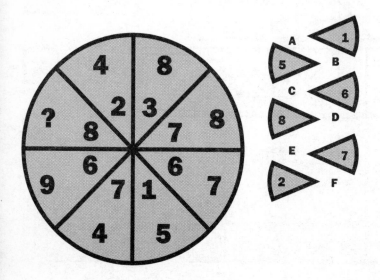

TEST 6

24 Which of the boxes should be used to replace the question mark?

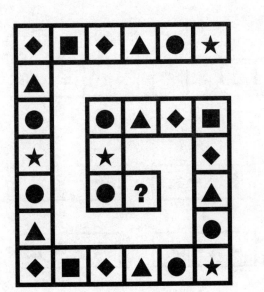

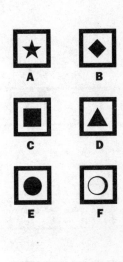

TEST 6

25 Insert the correct mathematical signs between each number in order to resolve the equation. What are the signs?

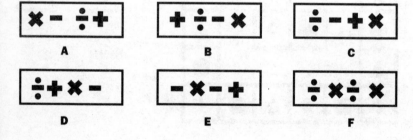

| 8 | | 7 | | 3 | | 1 | | 19 | = | 76 |

× − ÷ +

A

+ ÷ − ×

B

÷ − + ×

C

÷ + × −

D

− × − +

E

÷ × ÷ ×

F

TEST 6

26 Here is an unusual safe. Each of the buttons must be pressed only once in the correct order to open it. The last button is marked F. The number of moves and the direction is marked on each button. Thus 1U would mean one move up, while 1Lwould mean one move to the left. Using the grid reference, which button is the first you must press?

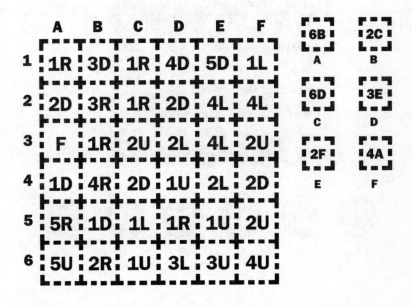

	A	B	C	D	E	F
1	1R	3D	1R	4D	5D	1L
2	2D	3R	1R	2D	4L	4L
3	F	1R	2U	2L	4L	2U
4	1D	4R	2D	1U	2L	2D
5	5R	1D	1L	1R	1U	2U
6	5U	2R	1U	3L	3U	4U

A 6B
B 2C
C 6D
D 3E
E 2F
F 4A

TEST 6

27 Move from ring to touching ring, starting from the bottom left corner and finishing in the top right corner. Collect nine numbers and total them. Which is the highest possible total?

TEST 6 time limit 45 minutes

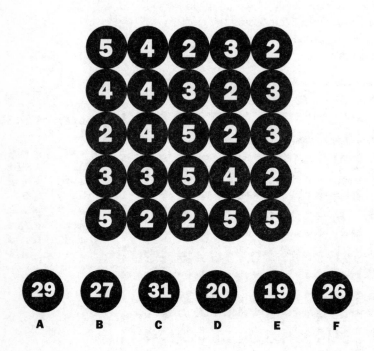

TEST 6

28 Which square's contents matches B1?

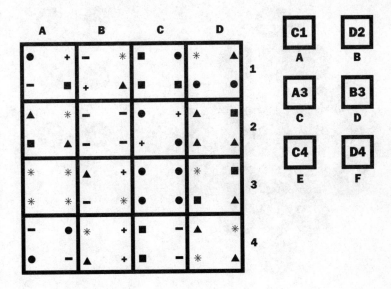

TEST 6

29 Which arrow is missing from this series?

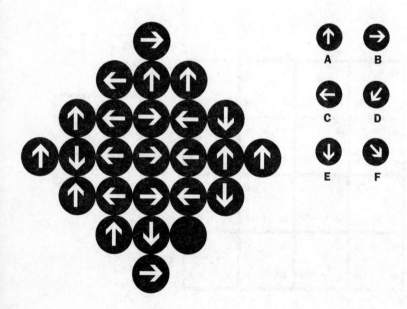

TEST 6

30 How many ways are there to score 58 on this dartboard using four darts only? Each dart always lands in a sector and no dart falls to the floor.

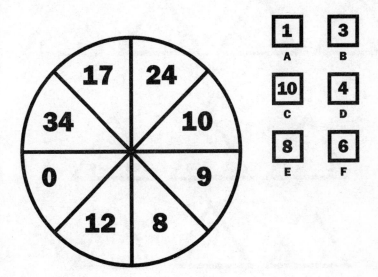

TEST 7

1 Which triangle belongs to this series?

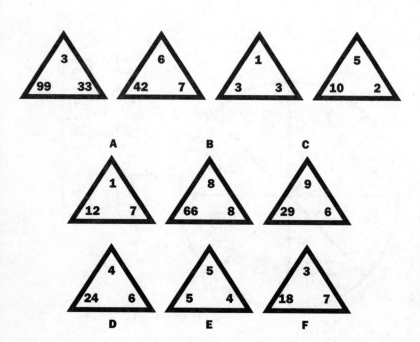

138

TEST 7

2 Start at 15 and move from circle to touching circle. Collect four numbers each time. How many different routes are there to collect 50? A reversed route counts twice.

10

10 10 5

10 20 20 5 20

5 20 10 15 5 5 20

20 10 10 10 10

5 20 5

5

5   2
A   B

3   6
C   D

7   8
E   F

TEST 7

3 Which of the numbers should replace the question mark?

2	2	5	7	0
4	9	5	7	?
7	2	1	4	6

1 A	**3** B
8 C	**9** D
6 E	**4** F

TEST 7

4 Which of the numbers should logically replace the question mark in the octagon?

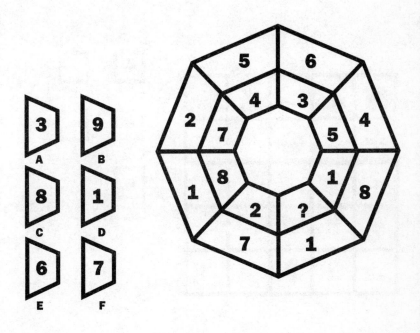

TEST 7

5   Complete the square using the five symbols shown. When completed no row, column or diagonal line will use the same symbol more than once. What should replace the question mark?

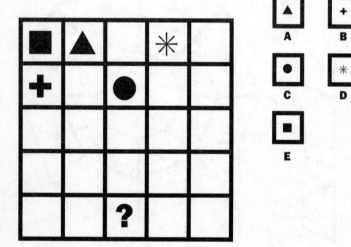

TEST 7

6 Here is an unusual safe. Each of the buttons must be pressed only once in the correct order to open it. The last button is marked F. The number of moves and the direction is marked on each button. Thus 1U would mean one move up, whilst 1L would mean one move to the left. Using the grid reference, which button is the first you must press?

	A	B	C	D	E	F
1	F	4D	6D	2L	2D	5L
2	4D	2R	3D	2R	4L	4D
3	2D	3D	2U	3L	1R	3L
4	4R	1U	1R	3U	2D	3U
5	1U	1U	1R	2U	2D	1L
6	3R	1R	4U	1D	5U	1U
7	1R	5U	2L	2R	5U	3U

2B **A**	7D **B**
1F **C**	4C **D**
6A **E**	3E **F**

TEST 7

7 Which of the boxes should be used to replace the question mark?

TEST 7 time limit 1 hour

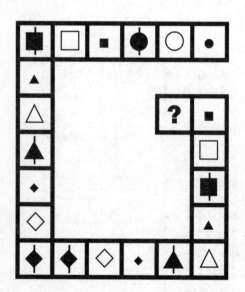

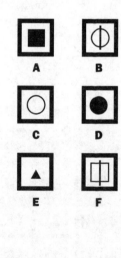

TEST 7

8 Which of the numbers should replace the question mark?

8	4	2	2	4
9	1	1	2	2
?	2	1	0	2

9
A

3
B

6
C

5
D

8
E

7
F

TEST 7

9 When rearranged the shapes will give a letter. Which of the letters is it?

TEST 7 time limit 1 hour

U A	W B
V C	N D
B E	C F

TEST 7

10 When the tiles in this square are rearranged a logical pattern will emerge. Which of the tiles should be used to complete the square?

3	1	1	2	2
3	1	2	1	1
3		1	1	2
1		2	2	3
2	3	2	2	2

A	B
2 3	2 2

C	D
4 1	1 1

E	F
1 4	5 1

TEST 7

11 How many ways are there to score 99 on this dartboard using five darts only? Each dart always lands in a sector and no dart falls to the floor.

TEST 7 time limit 1 hour

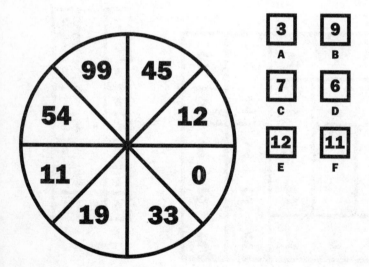

TEST 7

12 Which square's contents matches A4?

TEST 7 time limit 1 hour

	A	B	C	D
1	+ ■ * ● ▲ −	■ ● − + * ■	● * + + ■ ▲	● + − − * ■
2	* ● + + ■ −	− * ■ + − −	* − * ▲ ● +	− + + ▲ ● *
3	▲ − * − + ●	● + * − ▲ ●	■ ● ■ ● ■ ●	+ ■ + ● ▲ −
4	+ ● * ▲ * −	− * ■ + + ▲	− ● − + ■ ▲	+ * * * ▲ ■

D3 A	**B4** B
C2 C	**A1** D
B1 E	**A3** F

149

TEST 7

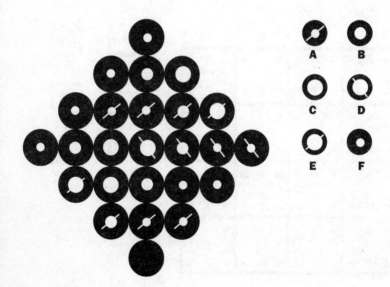

13 Which shape is missing from this series?

TEST 7 time limit 1 hour

TEST 7

14 Which triangle should replace the empty one?

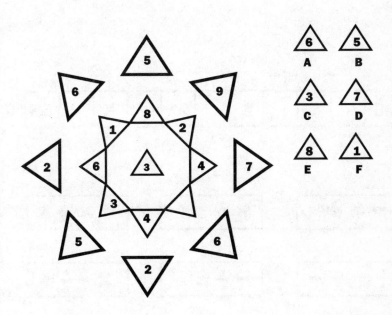

TEST 7

Insert the correct mathematical signs between each number in order to resolve the equation. What are the signs?

TEST 7 time limit 1 hour

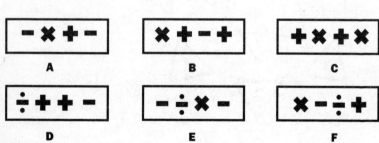

| 28 | | 4 | | 8 | | 21 | | 5 | = | 58 |

− ✕ + −
A

✕ + − +
B

+ ✕ + ✕
C

÷ + + −
D

− ÷ ✕ −
E

✕ − ÷ +
F

152

TEST 7

16 Which of the constructed boxes cannot be made from the pattern?

TEST 7 time limit 1 hour

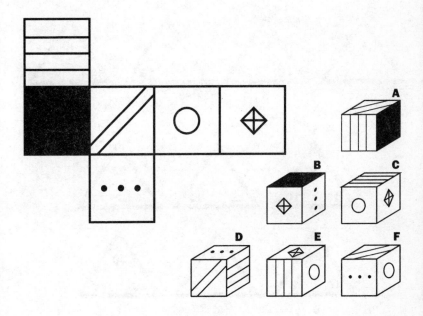

TEST 7

17 Which triangle continues this series?

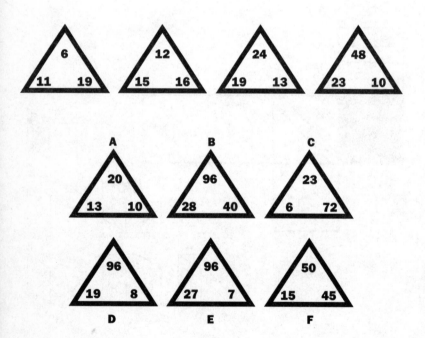

TEST 7

18 Which of the slices should be used to complete the cake?

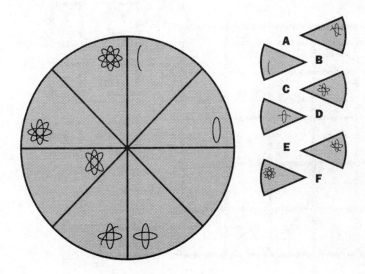

TEST 7

19 Each straight line of five numbers should total 45. Which of the numbers will replace the question mark?

11	12	13	0	
8	13	13	11	0
11	13			3
6				
	0	?	24	

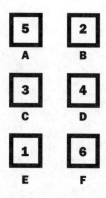

A 5 B 2

C 3 D 4

E 1 F 6

TEST 7

20 Here is an unusual safe. Each of the buttons must be pressed only once in the correct order to open it. The last button is marked F. The number of moves and the direction is marked on each button. Thus 1i would mean one move in, whilst 1o would mean one move out. 1c would mean one move clockwise and 1a would mean one move anti-clockwise. Which button is the first you must press?

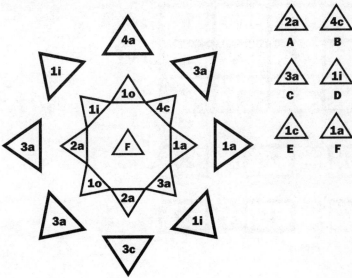

21 Each same symbol has a value. Work out the logic and discover what should replace the question mark.

φ	φ	φ	γ	?
γ	γ	γ	η	29
τ	τ	τ	η	68
η	η	φ	γ	
41			30	

35 A	**20** B	**25** C
27 D	**31** E	**32** F

TEST 7

22 This square follows a logical pattern. Which of the tiles should be used to complete the square?

TEST 7 time limit 1 hour

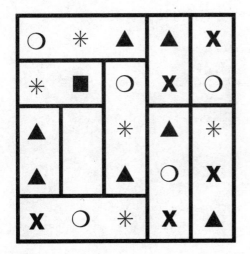

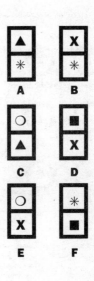

TEST 7

23 When rearranged the shapes will give a number. Which of the numbers is it?

TEST 7 time limit 1 hour

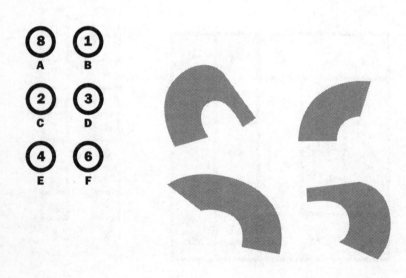

TEST 7

24 Scales one and two are in perfect balance. Which of these pans should replace the empty one?

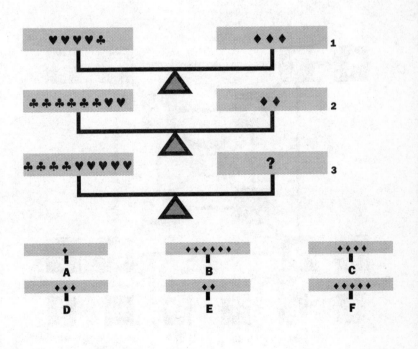

TEST 7

25 Start at any corner and follow the lines. Collect another four numbers and total the five. One of the numbers in the squares below can be used to complete the diagram. If the correct one has been chosen, one of the routes involving it will give a total of 45. Which one is it?

TEST 7 time limit 1 hour

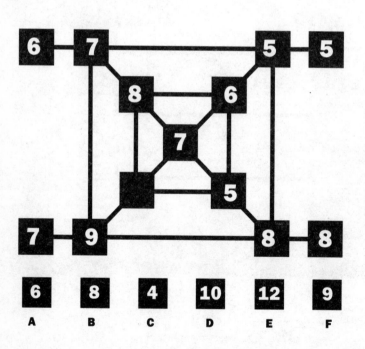

TEST 7

26 Which of the numbers should replace the question mark?

A	B	C	D
4	2	7	1
1	9	5	4
3	5	8	7
2	7	6	?

8	2
A	B
9	1
C	D
6	5
E	F

TEST 7

27 Insert the correct mathematical signs between each number in order to resolve the equation. What are the signs?

TEST 7 time limit 1 hour

| 9 | | 4 | | 2 | | 17 | | 16 | = | 18 |

A + ÷ − ×

B × × ÷ ÷

C ÷ × − +

D × − ÷ +

E + + − ×

F − − × +

TEST 7

28 Which of the constructed boxes can be made from the pattern?

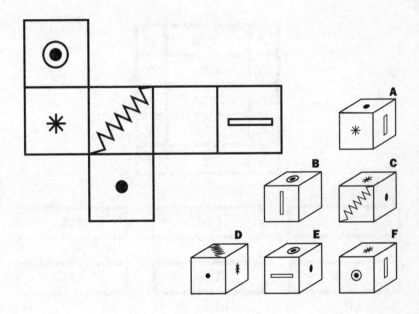

TEST 7

29 Discover the connection between the letters and the numbers. Which number should replace the question mark?

F	136	M
U	421	D
H	178	Q
O	115	A
X	?	I

672	834	411
A	B	C

295	118	924
D	E	F

TEST 7

30 Which of the clocks continues this series?

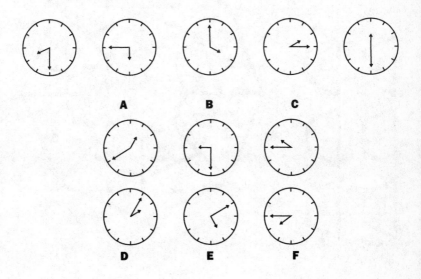

TEST 8

1 Which of the numbers should logically replace the question mark in the octagon?

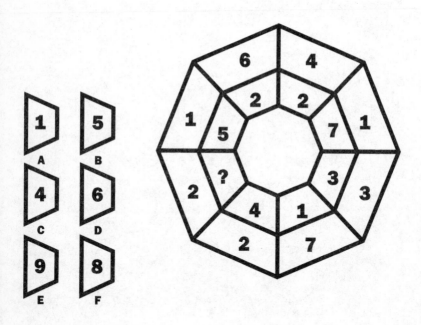

TEST 8

2 Complete the square using the five numbers shown. When completed no row, column or diagonal line will use the same number more than once. Which can logically replace the question mark?

5	2	4	3	
1				
		?		

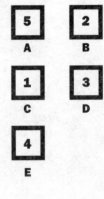

5   A

2   B

1   C

3   D

4   E

TEST 8

3 Start at 3 and move from circle to touching circle. Collect four numbers each time. How many different routes are there to collect 13? A reversed route counts twice.

```
                    5
                 5  4  5
              1  1  1  5  4
           1  4  1  3  5  5  1
              4  4  4  1  1
                 5  4  1
                    4
```

```
   1        5
   A        B

   3        6
   C        D

   7        4
   E        F
```

TEST 8

4 Which of the numbers should replace the question mark?

9	5	4	8	1
8	9	6	3	1
7	5	?	2	3

3	2
A	B
6	9
C	D
5	1
E	F

TEST 8

5   Here is an unusual safe. Each of the buttons must be pressed only once in the correct order to open it. The last button is marked F. The number of moves and the direction is marked on each button. Thus 1i would mean one move in, while 1o would mean one move out. 1c would mean one move clockwise and 1a would mean one move anti-clockwise. Which button is the first you must press?

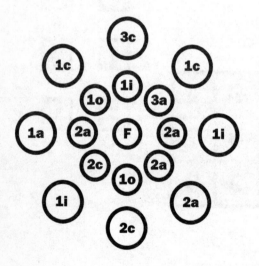

TEST 8

6 Which of the boxes should be used to replace the question mark?

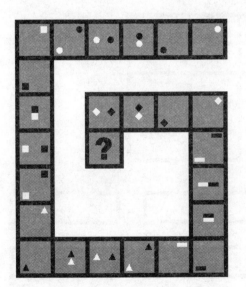

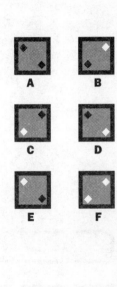

TEST 8

7 Discover the connection between the letters and the numbers. Which number should replace the question mark?

TEST 8 time limit 1 hour

K	16
Y	2
P	11
E	22
L	?

15	**13**	**11**
A	B	C
18	**8**	**6**
D	E	F

TEST 8

8 Which of the clocks continues this series?

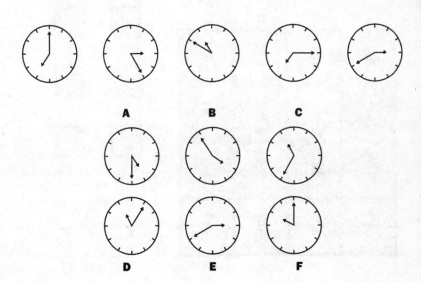

A   B   C

D   E   F

TEST 8

9 Which of the numbers should replace the question mark?

	A	B	C	D
	7	5	3	4
	9	7	2	8
	6	8	7	2
	4	5	3	?

4	7
A	B

3	9
C	D

6	8
E	F

TEST 8

10 Each same symbol has a value.
Work out the logic and discover what
should replace the question mark.

TEST 8 time limit 1 hour

τ	ψ	η	φ	63
φ	η	ψ	ψ	
τ	τ	τ	ψ	85
η	φ	η	η	?
58	63	61		

33	A		30	B		38	C

31	D		36	E		34	F

TEST 8

11 Move from ring to touching ring, starting from the bottom left corner and finishing in the top right corner. Collect nine numbers and total them. Which is the highest possible total?

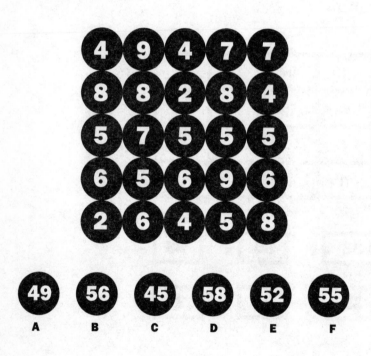

4	9	4	7	7
8	8	2	8	4
5	7	5	5	5
6	5	6	9	6
2	6	4	5	8

| 49 | 56 | 45 | 58 | 52 | 55 |
| A | B | C | D | E | F |

TEST 8

12 Scales one and two are in perfect balance. Which of these pans should replace the empty one?

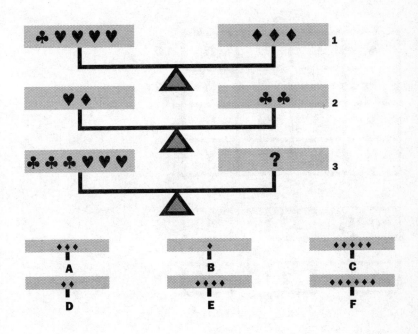

179

TEST 8

13 Each same letter has a value.
Work out the logic and discover what
should replace the question mark.

V	V	B	N	60
H	H	N	B	32
V	B	N	B	
N	H	V	V	66
	40	?		

40	A	35	B	49	C

38	D	52	E	50	F

TEST 8

14 Here is an unusual safe. Each of the buttons must be pressed only once in the correct order to open it. The last button is marked F. The number of moves and the direction is marked on each button. Thus 1U would mean one move up, while 1L would mean one move to the left. Using the grid reference, which button is the first you must press?

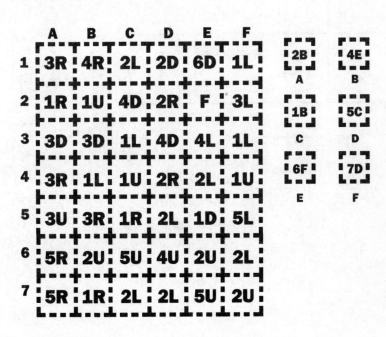

	A	B	C	D	E	F
1	3R	4R	2L	2D	6D	1L
2	1R	1U	4D	2R	F	3L
3	3D	3D	1L	4D	4L	1L
4	3R	1L	1U	2R	2L	1U
5	3U	3R	1R	2L	1D	5L
6	5R	2U	5U	4U	2U	2L
7	5R	1R	2L	2L	5U	2U

2B	4E
A	B

1B	5C
C	D

6F	7D
E	F

TEST 8

15 Which of the constructed boxes can be made from the pattern?

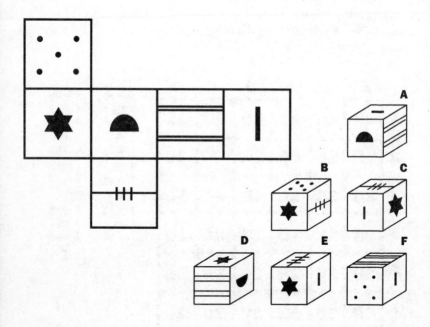

TEST 8

16 When rearranged the shapes will give a number. Which of the numbers is it?

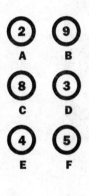

(2) A

(9) B

(8) C

(3) D

(4) E

(5) F

TEST 8

17 Move from ring to touching ring, starting from the bottom left corner and finishing in the top right corner. Collect nine numbers and total them. Which is the highest possible total?

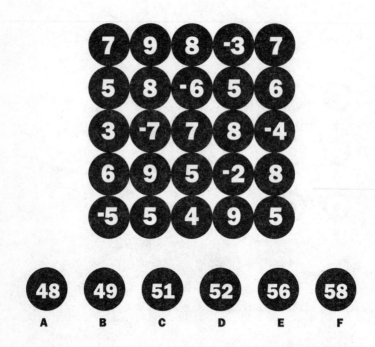

TEST 8

18 Which of the boxes should be used to replace the question mark?

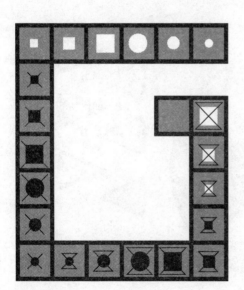

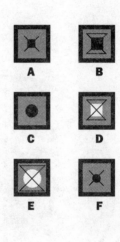

185

TEST 8

19 Which of the slices should be used to complete the cake so that the top half matches the bottom half?

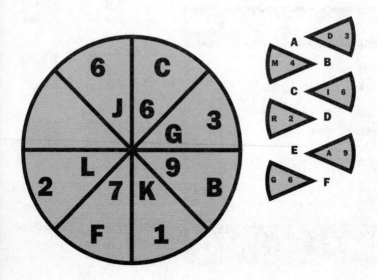

TEST 8

20 Which square's contents matches D2?

	A	B	C	D	
	■ 3 C	D ▲ 3	3 C D	■ ■ ■	1
	D ▲ 1	D 1 D	C ▲ ▲	3 3 3	
	1 3 1	C C 1	▲ ■ 1	3 ▲ C	2
	■ ■ ■	D D ■	1 1 1	▲ ■ 3	
	C 3 3	3 ▲ 3	C 3 C	▲ 3 3	3
	▲ ■ ▲	▲ 1 ▲	▲ C 1	3 ▲ C	
	■ ■ 1	▲ C ▲	1 C ▲	1 C 3	4
	▲ C 1	▲ D ▲	■ ▲ 1	■ 1 ■	

D4 A	**C1** B
B1 C	**B2** D
A3 E	**C2** F

TEST 8

21 When the tiles in this square are rearranged a logical pattern will emerge. Which of the tiles should be used to complete the square?

9	1	6	5	
9	6	3	4	
9	8	1	6	8
1	2	7	7	7
2	9	5	2	3

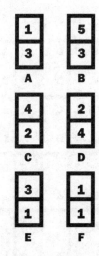

TEST 8

22 Discover the connection between the letters and the numbers. Which number should replace the question mark?

W	4	S
J	6	D
O	3	L
R	10	H
V	?	K

4	16	8
A	B	C

11	3	15
D	E	F

TEST 8

23 Here is an unusual safe. Each of the buttons must be pressed only once in the correct order to open it. The last button is marked F. The number of moves and the direction is marked on each button. Thus 1i would mean one move in, while 1o would mean one move out. 1c would mean one move clockwise and 1a would mean one move anti-clockwise. Which button is the first you must press?

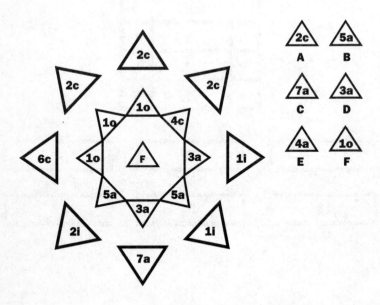

TEST 8

24 Which of the clocks continues
this series?

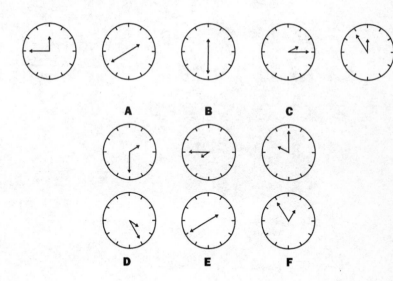

TEST 8

25 Start at 2 and move from circle to touching circle. Collect four numbers each time. How many different routes are there to collect 39? A reversed route counts twice.

TEST 8 time limit 1 hour

16

13 13 8

13 13 16 13 16

16 8 13 2 8 8 8

13 13 13 16 16

16 8 16

13

5	10
A	B

8	9
C	D

6	7
E	F

TEST 8

26 Scales one and two are in perfect balance. Which of these pans should replace the empty one?

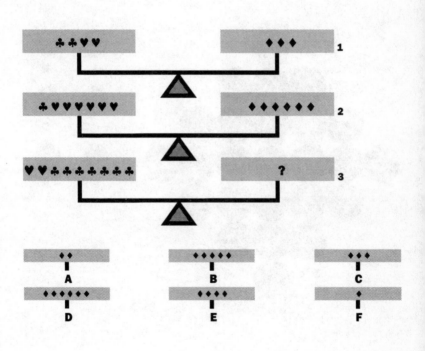

TEST 8

27 Which shape is missing from this series?

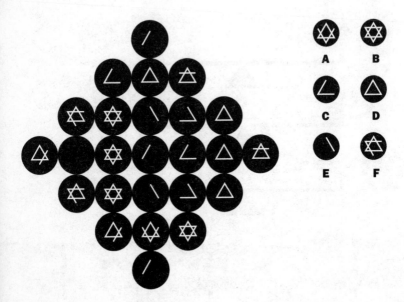

TEST 8

28 Which circle should replace the empty one?

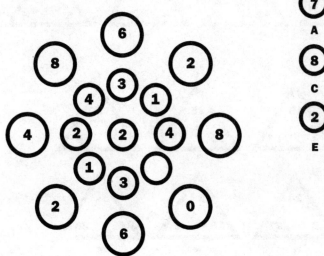

195

TEST 8

29 Which triangle continues this series?

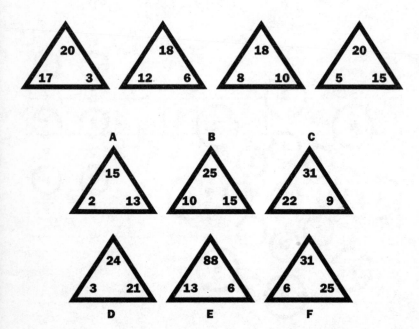

First row of triangles:
- 20 / 17 3
- 18 / 12 6
- 18 / 8 10
- 20 / 5 15

Answer options:

A 15 / 2 13

B 25 / 10 15

C 31 / 22 9

D 24 / 3 21

E 88 / 13 6

F 31 / 6 25

TEST 8

30 Insert the correct mathematical signs between each number in order to resolve the equation. What are the signs?

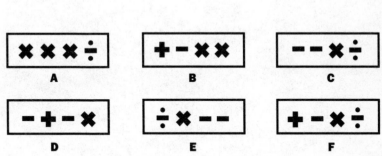

| 53 | | 35 | | 2 | | 4 | | 16 | = | 4 |

× × × ÷
A

+ − × ×
B

− − × ÷
C

− + − ×
D

÷ × − −
E

+ − × ÷
F

ANSWERS

TESTS 1 – 8

TEST 1 ANSWERS

1 F. On each row A + B + C = D.

2 D. $\Omega=5$, $\Xi=2$, $\Psi=4$, $Z=3$.

3 F.

4 E.

5 B. The numbers in the first triangle total 3, the second 4 and so on.

6 B. The alphabetical value of each letter is placed next to it.

7 C.

8 C. Each row totals 10.

9 B. The hour hand moves forward two hours each time.

10 E.

11 F.

12 D. When completed the box reads the same both down and across.

13 C.

14 D.

15 F.

TEST 1 ANSWERS

SCORE	I.Q.	PERCENTILE
15	130	90
14	125	85
13	122	80
12	117	75
11	115	70
10	112	65
9	108	60
8	105	55
7	100	50
6	95	45
5	90	40

TEST 2 ANSWERS

1 F.

2 A. ♣ = 6, ♥ = 5, ♦ = 2.

3 F.

4 E.

5 C. Each double section totals 10.

6 B. Two series lead from 1 to 16.

7 C.

8 D. Deduct row 2 from row 1 to give row 3.

9 C.

10 E.

11 E. On each row the two squares to the left total 9, as do the two to the right.

12 F. The numbers in the triangles total 4, 6, 8, 10 etc.

13 C.

14 A. The alphabetical value of each letter is placed next to it.

15 A.

TEST 2 ANSWERS

SCORE	I.Q.	PERCENTILE
15	130	90
14	125	85
13	122	80
12	117	75
11	115	70
10	112	65
9	108	60
8	105	55
7	100	50
6	95	45
5	90	40

TEST 3 ANSWERS

1 C. $\alpha=4$, $\beta=7$, $\chi=5$, $\delta=8$.

2 A. ♣ = 2, ♥ = 1, ♦ = 3.

3 E.

4 B. Each of the four columns of numbers totals 15.

5 C. 4a in the inner ring.

6 D. The numbers on each row total 9.

7 A. A large triangle added to the nearest small triangle will give the middle number.

8 E. Each double section is added together. Reading clockwise from 2 + 1, the totals increase by one each time.

9 B.

10 E.

11 D.

12 F. Each double section totals 13.

13 A. On each row the first figure minus the second figure plus the third figure gives the fourth.

14 E.

15 E. The first row plus the second row gives the third row.

16 C. The box now reads the same down and across.

17 B.

18 E.

19 E. ♣ = 8, ♥ = 6, ♦ = 7.

20 D. The hour hand moves forward two hours, then three hours, then four hours etc.

TEST 3 ANSWERS

SCORE	I.Q.	PERCENTILE
20	138	95
19	136	94
18	134	93
17	132	92
16	131	91
15	130	90
14	125	85
13	122	80
12	117	75
11	115	70
10	112	65
9	108	60
8	105	55
7	100	50
6	95	45
5	90	40

TEST 4 ANSWERS

1 A.

2 B.

3 B. In each triangle the bottom two numbers, when added together, give the top number.

4 F. The hour hand moves back four hours each time.

5 C. On each row $A + B - C = D$.

6 E.

7 D.

8 A. When completed the box reads the same both down and across.

9 C.

10 C.

11 D.

12 D.

13 A. $\alpha=6$, $\beta=3$, $\chi=7$, $\delta=10$.

14 B.

15 D.

16 F. A large circle minus the nearest small circle will give the middle number.

17 A.

18 B. Reading clockwise, the numbers relate to the number of line forming the shape in the previous sector.

19 C. The first row plus the third row gives the second row. in the middle.

20 E. The alphabetical positions of the letters are placed together in the middle.

TEST 4 ANSWERS

SCORE	I.Q.	PERCENTILE
20	138	95
19	136	94
18	134	93
17	132	92
16	131	91
15	130	90
14	125	85
13	122	80
12	117	75
11	115	70
10	112	65
9	108	60
8	105	55
7	100	50
6	95	45
5	90	40

TEST 5 ANSWERS

1 B. 2c in the inner ring.

2 B.

3 A. Reading clockwise, the number in the sector is the alphabetical value of the letter in the previous sector.

4 F.

5 F.

6 C. Each column totals 8.

7 E.

8 B. From the 1, the numbers increase in a spiral by missing out one number, then two numbers, then three numbers and so on.

9 C.

10 F.

11 B. Each double section is added together. These totals increase by two each time.

12 F. When completed the box reads the same both down and across.

13 D. The value of individual letters is irrelevant.
The total of the row of numbers must match the total of the column of numbers.

14 E.

15 A.

TEST 5 ANSWERS

16 E. On each row A - B - C = D.

17 B.

18 C. ♣ = 4, ♥ = 3, ♦ = 1.

19 D. 1o in the inner ring, between another 1o and 5a.

20 F.

21 A. The left number plus the top number gives the right number in each triangle.

22 C. The alphabetical values of the letters are added to give the number in the middle space.

23 B. The minute hand moves forward ten minutes and the hour hand one hour on each clock.

24 F. Divide the square into four 2 x 2 blocks. The four numbers in each block total 20.

25 D.

26 A.

27 F.

28 A.

29 A.

30 E.

TEST 5 ANSWERS

SCORE	I.Q.	PERCENTILE
30	161	99
29	160	99
28	157	99
27	155	99
26	154	98
25	152	98
24	150	98
23	148	98*
22	143	97
21	140	96
20	138	95
19	136	94
18	134	93
17	132	92
16	131	91
15	130	90
14	125	85
13	122	80
12	117	75
11	115	70
10	112	65
9	108	60
8	105	55
7	100	50
6	95	45
5	90	40

* MENSA LEVEL
You should attempt to join
– see front page for details.

TEST 6 ANSWERS

1 E. The sectors in the bottom half total one higher than their opposite in the top half.

2 C.

3 F.

4 B.

5 F. 2c in the inner ring with 2c on either side, and 2c outside.

6 D. ♣ = 5, ♥ = 7, ♦ = 4.

7 F.

8 F. The third row plus the second row gives the first row.

9 A. Start in the extreme left circle. The series of arrows zigzags up and down with the arrows pointing as follows: up, down, right, left, down. This repeats.

10 D.

11 B. When completed the box shows the same pattern both down and across.

12 F.

13 C.

14 A. Each double section is added together. This double and its opposite have the same total.

15 E. The middle circle and the two rings of circles all total 24.

TEST 6 ANSWERS

16 D.

17 E. The alphabetical positions of the letters are found and the smaller is taken from the larger.

18 C. In each triangle the bottom two numbers are multiplied to give the top.

19 B. K=11, Λ=12, O=15, Π=16.

20 D. On each row A x B + C = D.

21 E. The hour hand moves forward one hour and the minute hand moves five minutes back each time.

22 E.

23 B. Opposite sectors total the same.

24 D.

25 B.

26 B.

27 C.

28 D.

29 C. Start in the top circle. The series of arrowszigzags across in a downward direction withthe arrows pointing as follows: right, left,up, up, down, left. This repeats.

30 E.

TEST 6 ANSWERS

SCORE	I.Q.	PERCENTILE
30	161	99
29	160	99
28	157	99
27	155	99
26	154	98
25	152	98
24	150	98
23	148	98*
22	143	97
21	140	96
20	138	95
19	136	94
18	134	93
17	132	92
16	131	91
15	130	90
14	125	85
13	122	80
12	117	75
11	115	70
10	112	65
9	108	60
8	105	55
7	100	50
6	95	45
5	90	40

* MENSA LEVEL
You should attempt to join
– see front page for details.

TEST 7 ANSWERS

1 D. The left number divided by the top number gives the right number in each triangle.

2 A.

3 E. The first row plus the second row gives the third row.

4 C. Each double section is added together. All double sections total 9.

5 E.

6 D.

7 D.

8 A. Reverse each row of numbers. Add the second row to the third to give the first row.

9 B.

10 D. When completed the box reads the same both down and across.

11 C.

12 C.

13 F.

14 A. All straight lines of five triangles total 22.

15 E.

TEST 7 ANSWERS

16 D.

17 E. In each triangle the left number increases by four, the right number decreases by three and the number at the top doubles each time.

18 D.

19 E.

20 A. 2a in the inner ring, between 1o and 1i.

21 C. $\phi=6$, $\gamma=7$, $\eta=8$, $\tau=20$.

22 E. When completed the box shows the same pattern both down and across.

23 D.

24 C. ♣ = 1, ♥ = 8, ♦ = 11.

25 E.

26 A. On each row A x B - C = D.

27 D.

28 F.

29 F. The alphabetical values of the letters are placed on opposite sides in the middle space.

30 C. The minute hand moves forward fifteen minutes and the hour hand moves back two hours on each clock.

TEST 7 ANSWERS

SCORE	I.Q.	PERCENTILE
30	161	99
29	160	99
28	157	99
27	155	99
26	154	98
25	152	98
24	150	98
23	148	98*
22	143	97
21	140	96
20	138	95
19	136	94
18	134	93
17	132	92
16	131	91
15	130	90
14	125	85
13	122	80
12	117	75
11	115	70
10	112	65
9	108	60
8	105	55
7	100	50
6	95	45
5	90	40

* MENSA LEVEL
You should attempt to join
– see front page for details.

TEST 8 ANSWERS

1   D. Each double section is added together. Totals of opposite sections are equal.

2   C.

3   E.

4   F. Reverse each row of numbers. Add the first

    row to the second to give the third row.

5   C. 2a in the inner ring between 2a and 1o.

6   C.

7   A. Reverse the alphabet and give each letter its value. For example A=26, B = 25.

8   D. The minute hand moves forward twenty-five   minutes and the hour hand moves

back   four hours on each clock.

9   C. On each row A + B ÷ C = D.

10 F. η=8, φ=10, τ=20, ψ=25.

11 B.

12 E. ♣ = 7, ♥ = 5, ♦ = 9.

13 E. B=2, H=8, N=14, V=22.

14 D.

15 E.

TEST 8 ANSWERS

16 B.

17 A.

18 E.

19 C. Give the letters their value in the alphabet and add them to the numbers. The top half of the circle will total 50, as will the bottom half.

20 E.

21 C. When completed the box reads the same both down and across.

22 D. The alphabetical value of the letters to the right are subtracted from the left to give the number in the middle space.

23 D. 3a in the inner ring, with 5a on both sides.

24 A. The minute hand moves back five minutes,then ten minutes then fifteen and so on. The hour hand moves two forward, twoback, two forward and so on.

25 B.

26 D.♣ = 6, ♥ = 9, ♦ = 10.

27 A.

28 F. The number in the middle circle multi plied by the adjacent small circle gives the value in the large outer circle.

29 D. In each triangle the left number decreases by five, four, three, two and so on. The right number increases by three, four, five, six and so on. The number at the top is left plus right.

30 C.

TEST 8 ANSWERS

SCORE	I.Q.	PERCENTILE
30	161	99
29	160	99
28	157	99
27	155	99
26	154	98
25	152	98
24	150	98
23	148	98*
22	143	97
21	140	96
20	138	95
19	136	94
18	134	93
17	132	92
16	131	91
15	130	90
14	125	85
13	122	80
12	117	75
11	115	70
10	112	65
9	108	60
8	105	55
7	100	50
6	95	45
5	90	40

* MENSA LEVEL
You should attempt to join
– see front page for details.